AUDIO ACCESS INCLUDED

30 Easy Rock
GUITAR SOLOS

To access audio visit:
www.halleonard.com/mylibrary

Enter Code
7133-0457-6889-1745

ISBN 978-1-4950-6074-8

HAL•LEONARD®
CORPORATION
7777 W. BLUEMOUND RD. P.O. BOX 13819 MILWAUKEE, WI 53213

In Australia Contact:
Hal Leonard Australia Pty. Ltd.
4 Lentara Court
Cheltenham, Victoria, 3192 Australia
Email: ausadmin@halleonard.com.au

Visit Hal Leonard Online at
www.halleonard.com

GUITAR NOTATION LEGEND

Guitar music can be notated two different ways: on a *musical staff*, and in *tablature*.

THE MUSICAL STAFF shows pitches and rhythms and is divided by bar lines into measures. Pitches are named after the first seven letters of the alphabet.

TABLATURE graphically represents the guitar fingerboard. Each horizontal line represents a string, and each number represents a fret.

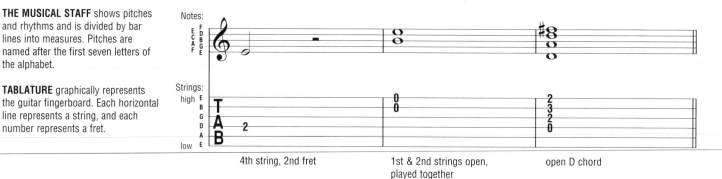

4th string, 2nd fret   1st & 2nd strings open, played together   open D chord

CHORD DIAGRAMS graphically represent the guitar fretboard to show correct chord fingerings.

- The letter above the diagram tells the name of the chord.
- The top, bold horizontal line represents the nut of the guitar. Each thin horizontal line represents a fret. Each vertical line represents a string; the low E string is on the far left and the high E string is on the far right.
- A dot shows where to put your fret-hand finger and the number at the bottom of the diagram tells which finger to use.
- The "O" above the string means play it open, while an "✕" means don't play the string.

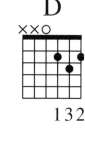

Definitions for Special Guitar Notation

HALF-STEP BEND: Strike the note and bend up 1/2 step.

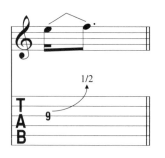

WHOLE-STEP BEND: Strike the note and bend up one step.

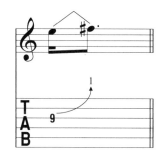

MUFFLED STRINGS: A percussive sound is produced by laying the fret hand across the string(s) without depressing, and striking them with the pick hand.

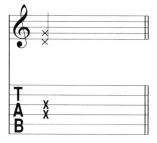

PALM MUTING: The note is partially muted by the pick hand lightly touching the string(s) just before the bridge.

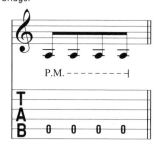

HAMMER-ON: Strike the first (lower) note with one finger, then sound the higher note (on the same string) with another finger by fretting it without picking.

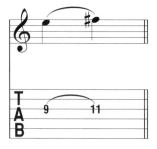

PULL-OFF: Place both fingers on the notes to be sounded. Strike the first note and without picking, pull the finger off to sound the second (lower) note.

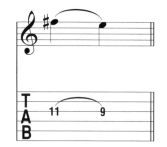

LEGATO SLIDE: Strike the first note and then slide the same fret-hand finger up or down to the second note. The second note is not struck.

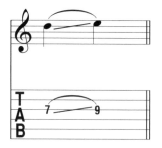

SHIFT SLIDE: Same as legato slide, except the second note is struck.

Additional Musical Definitions

Fill
- Label used to identify a brief melodic figure which is to be inserted into the arrangement.

D.S. al Coda
- Go back to the sign (𝄋), then play until the measure marked "***To Coda***," then skip to the section labelled "**Coda.**"

D.C. al Fine
- Go back to the beginning of the song and play until the measure marked "***Fine***" (end).

N.C.
- No chord. Instrument is silent.

- Repeat measures between signs.

- When a repeated section has different endings, play the first ending only the first time and the second ending only the second time.

Annie Laurie

Words by William Douglas
Music by Lady John Scott

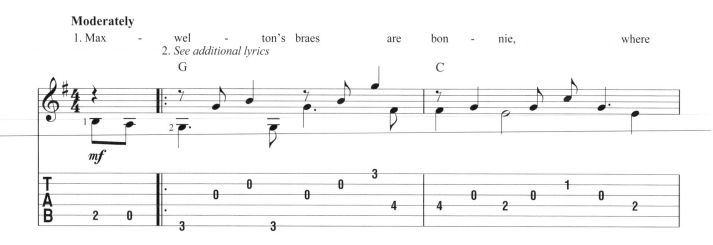

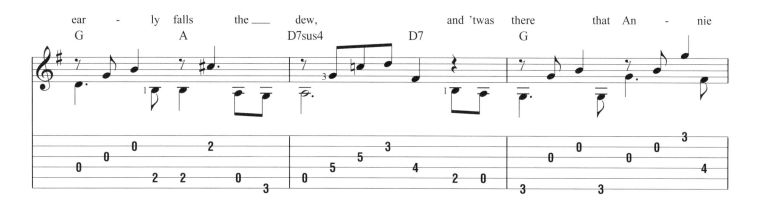

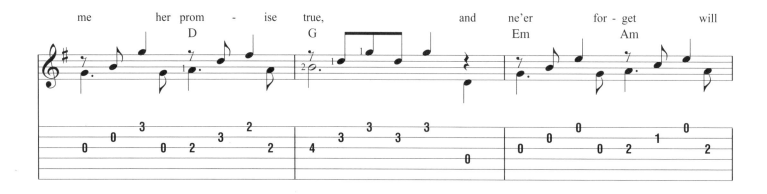

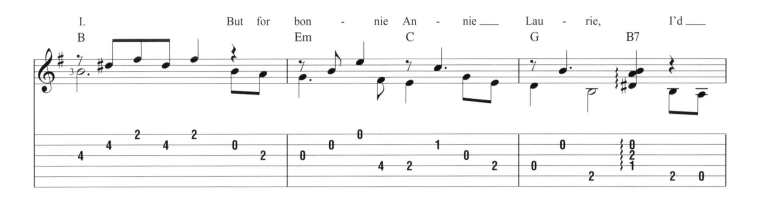

Additional Lyrics

2. Her brow is like the snowdrift, her neck is like the swan.
   Her face, it is the fairest that e'er the sun shone on,
   That e'er the sun shone on, and dark blue is her eye.
   But for bonny Annie Laurie, I'd lay me down and die.

Barbara Allen

Traditional English

Moderately, in 2

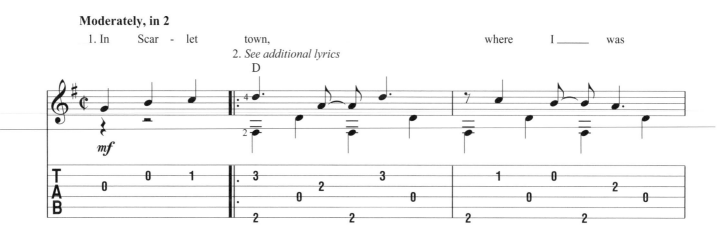

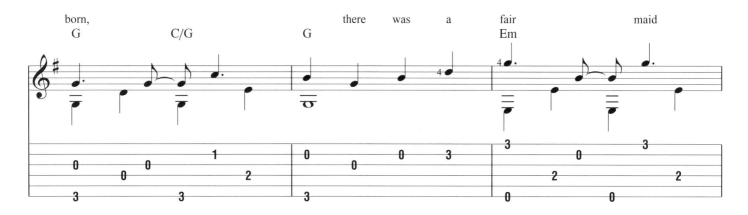

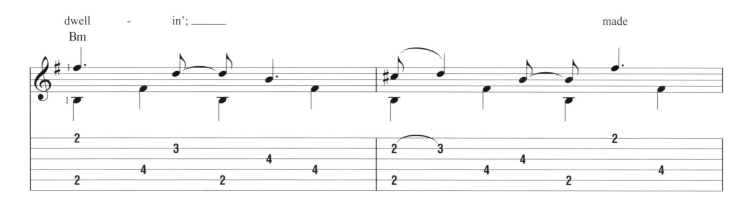

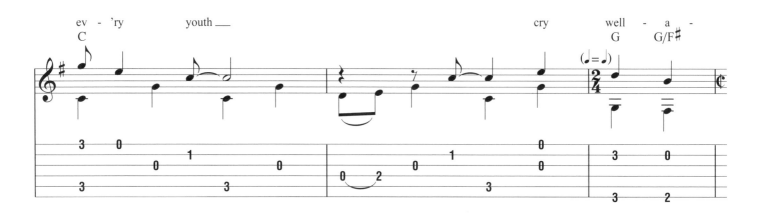

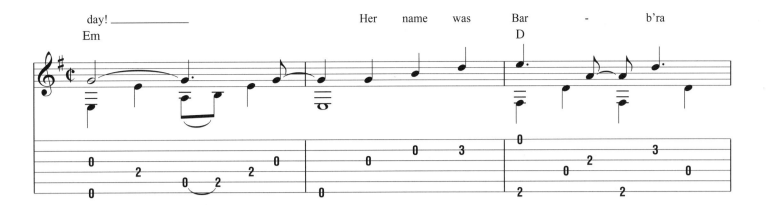

day! _____   Her   name   was   Bar   -   b'ra

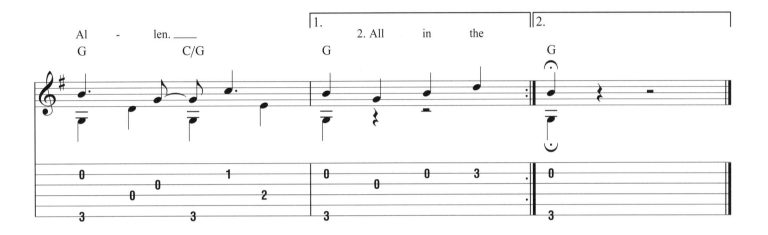

Al   -   len. ____   2. All   in   the

Additional Lyrics

2. All in the merry month of May,
   When green buds, they were swellin',
   Sweet William on his deathbed lay,
   For love of Barbara Allen.

Black Is the Color of My True Love's Hair

Southern Appalachian Folksong

Moderately

1. Black, black, black is the col-or of my true love's
2. *See additional lyrics*

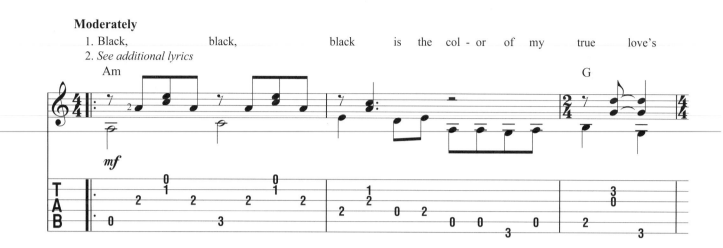

hair. _____ Her lips _____ are like some ros-y fiar; the _____

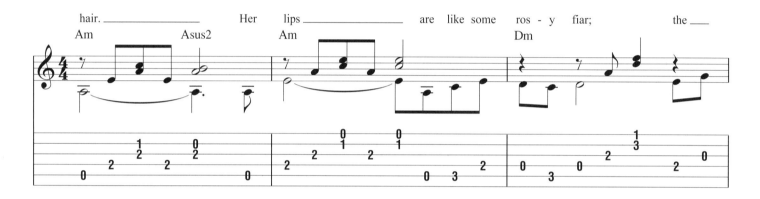

pur-est _____ eyes and the neat-est _____ hands. _____ I

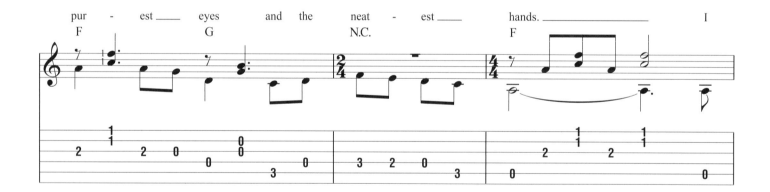

love _____ the grass where-on she stands.

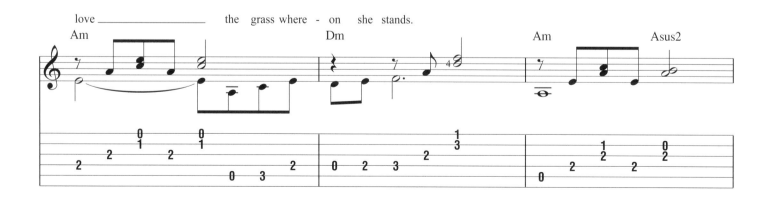

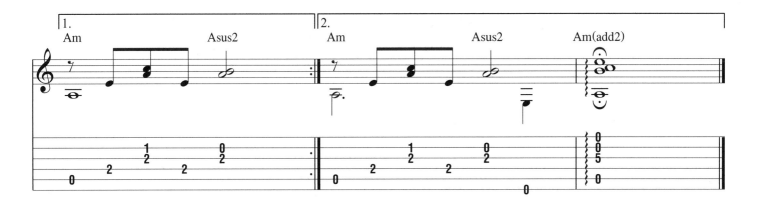

Additional Lyrics

2. Black, black, black is the color of my true love's hair.
   Her face is something truly rare.
   Oh, I do love my love and so well she knows.
   I love the ground whereon she goes.

Butcher Boy

Traditional Irish Folksong

Moderately, in 2

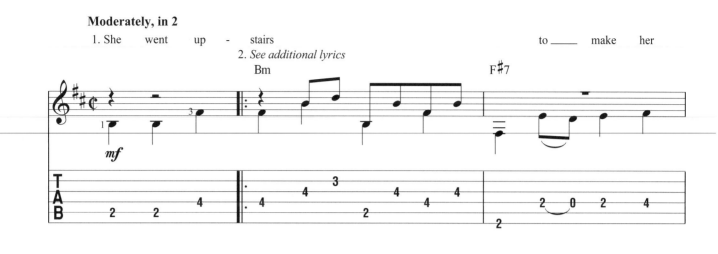

1. She went up-stairs to make her
2. *See additional lyrics*

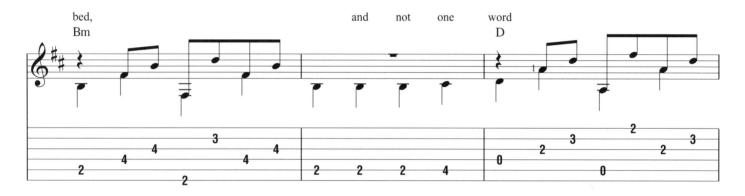

bed, and not one word

to her moth-er said. Her moth-er,

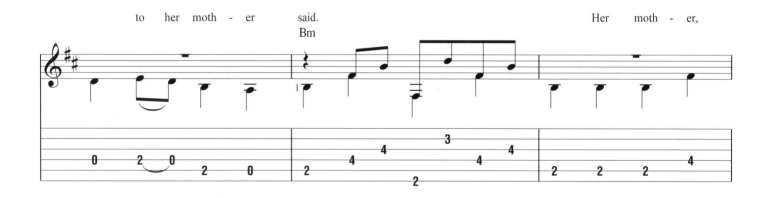

she went up-stairs too,

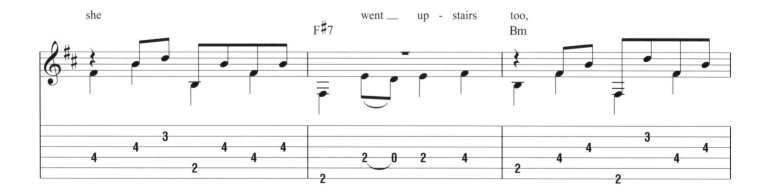

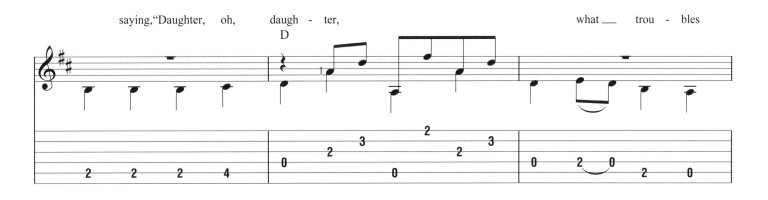

saying, "Daughter, oh, daugh - ter,   what ___ trou - bles

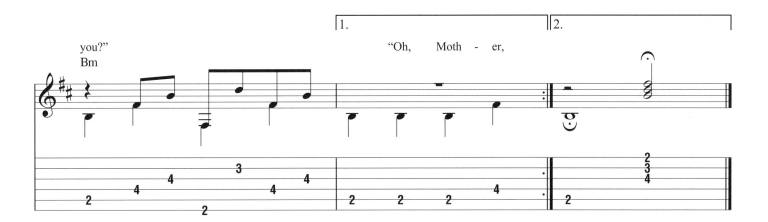

you?"   "Oh,   Moth - er,

Additional Lyrics

2. "Oh, Mother, dear, I cannot tell,
That butcher boy I love so well.
He courted me, my life away,
And now at home he will not stay."

Come All Ye Fair and Tender Maidens

Kentucky Folksong

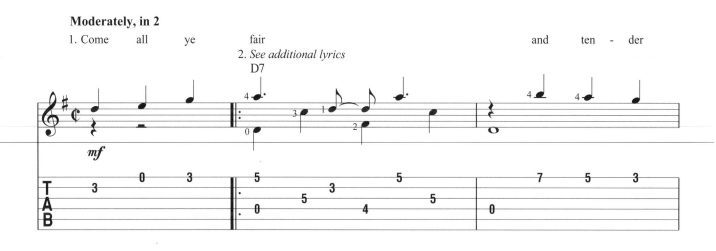

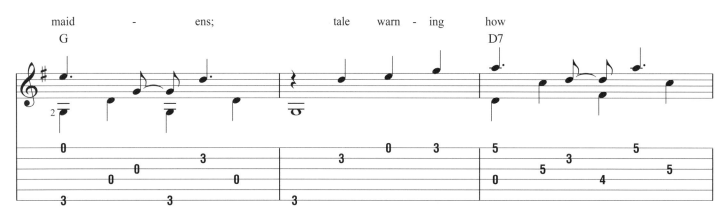

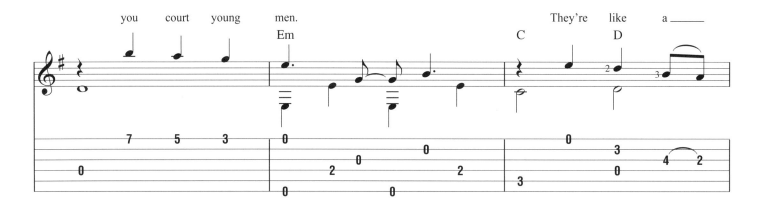

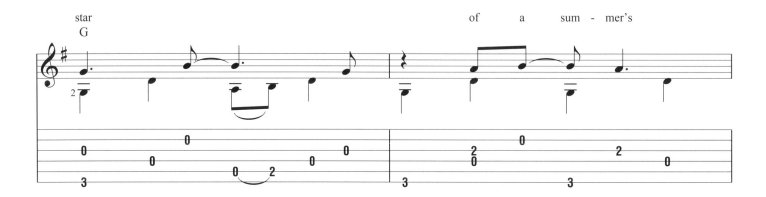

morn - ing: ___ first they'll ap - pear

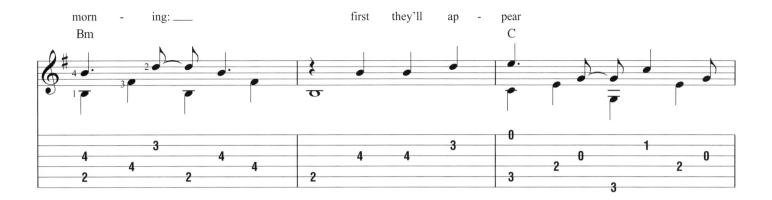

and then they're gone. 2. They win your

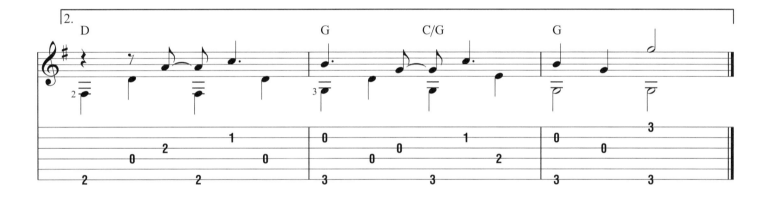

2. They win your heart with tender stories,

Additional Lyrics

2. They win your heart with tender stories,
And they'll declare their love so true.
And then they'll go and court some other,
And that's the love they have for you.

Down in the Valley

Traditional American Folksong

Drop D tuning:
(low to high) D-A-D-G-B-E

Moderately

1. Down in the val - ley,

2., 3., 4. *See additional lyrics*

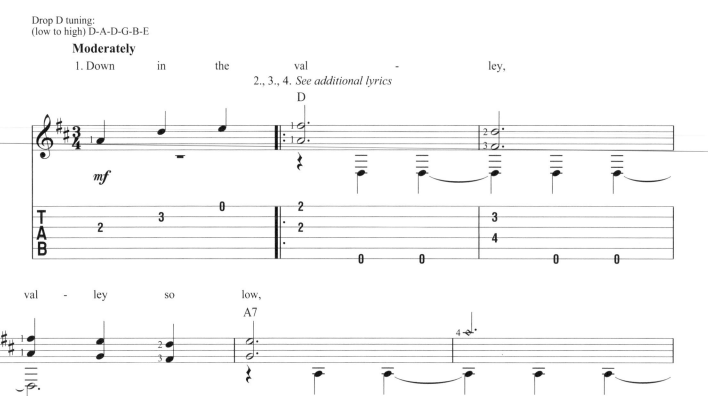

val - ley so low,

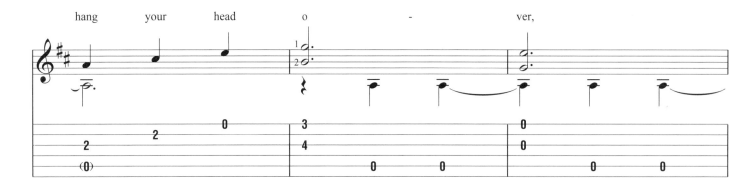

hang your head o - ver,

hear the wind blow.

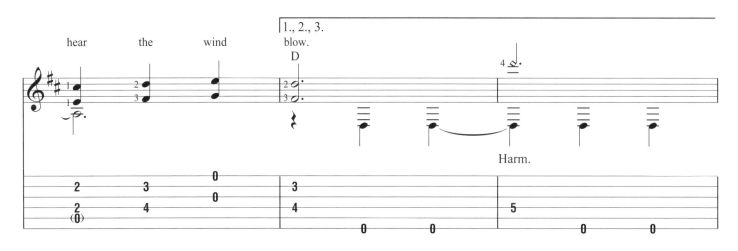

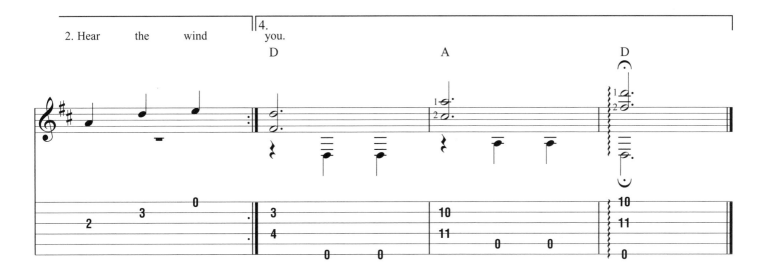

Additional Lyrics

2. Hear the wind blow, dear, hear the wind blow;
   Hang your head over, hear the wind blow.

3. Roses love sunshine, violets love dew;
   Angels in heaven know I love you.

4. Know I love you, dear, know I love you;
   Angels in heaven know I love you.

Fare Thee Well

English Folksong

Moderately, in 2

1. Oh, fare thee well, I _____ must be _____
2. *See additional lyrics*

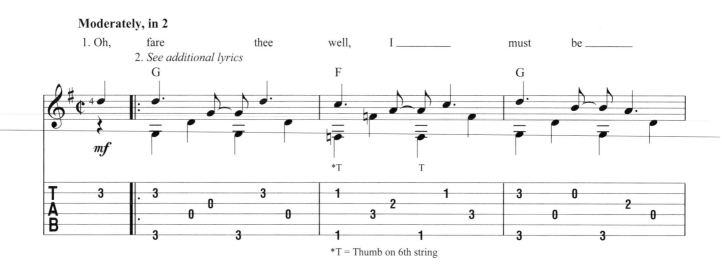

*T = Thumb on 6th string

gone _____ and leave you for a

while. Wher - ev - er _____ I

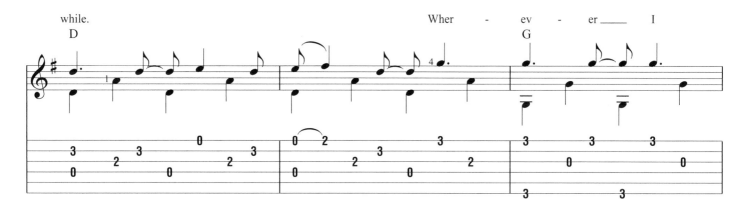

go, I will re - turn, if _____ I

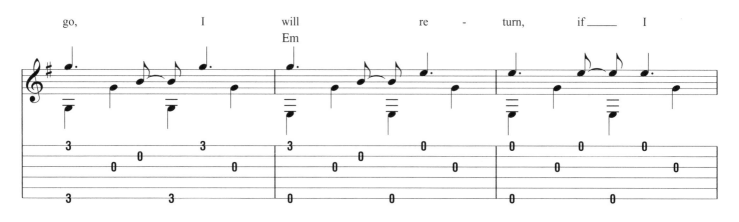

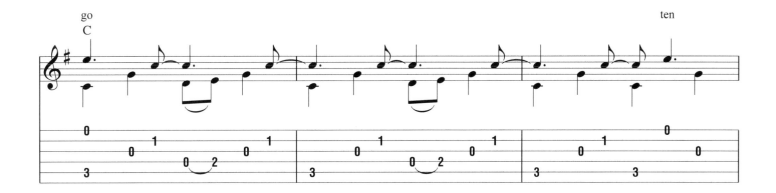

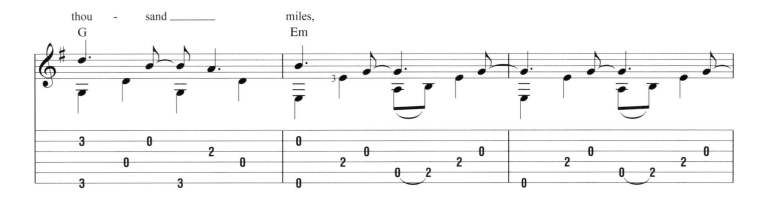

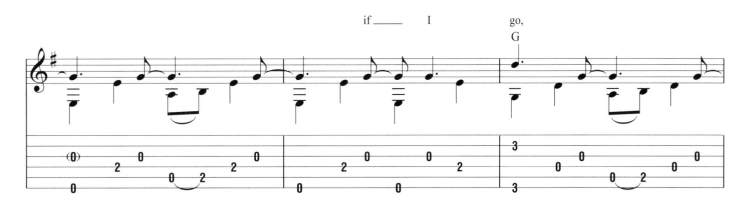

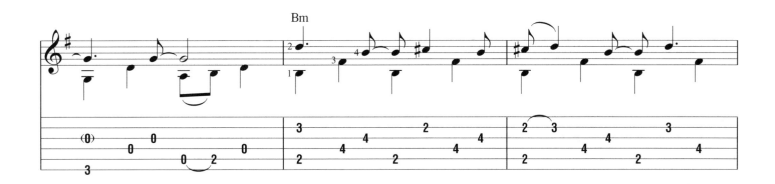

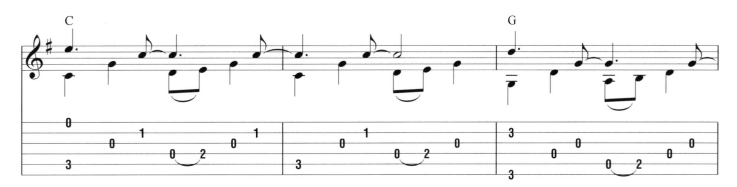

if ____ I go, Em

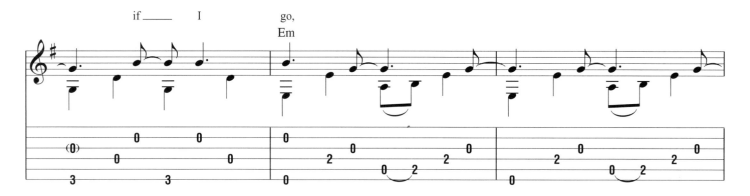

if ____ I go ten C

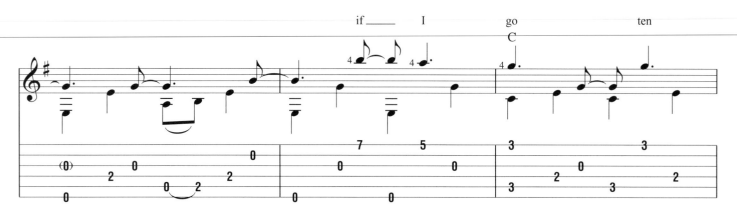

thou - sand miles. D G

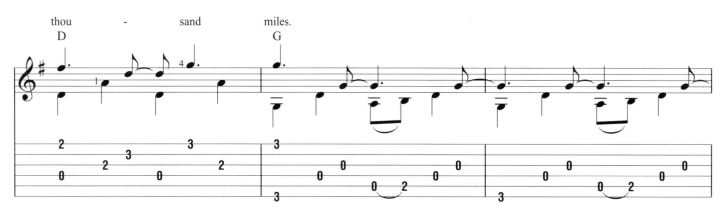

1.   2. Ten   2.

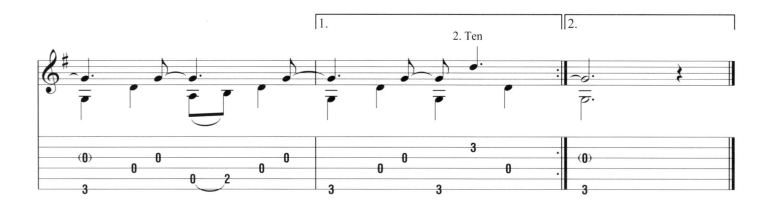

Additional Lyrics

2. Ten thousand miles, it is so far to leave me here alone,
While I may lie, lament and cry, and you'll not hear my moan,
And you, no, you, and you'll not hear my moan.

The Gallows Pole

Traditional Folksong

*T = Thumb on 6th string

Additional Lyrics

2. Papa, did you bring me silver? Did you bring me gold?
   Did you come to see me hangin' by the gallows pole?

3. "I couldn't bring no silver. I didn't bring no gold.
   I come to see you hangin' by the gallows pole."

4. Hangman, hangman, slack your rope; slack it for a while
   Think I see my sweetheart comin', ridin' many a mile.

Fennario

Scottish Folksong

Moderately, in 2

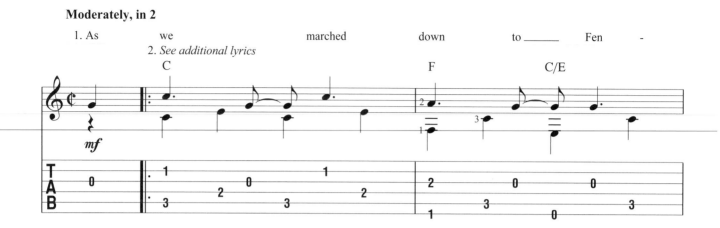

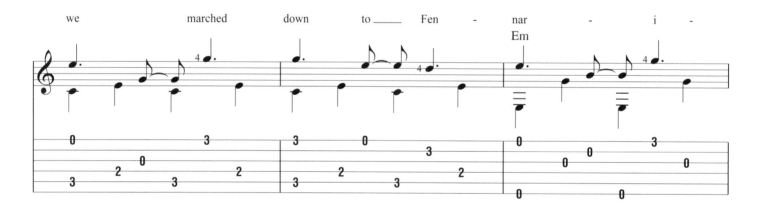

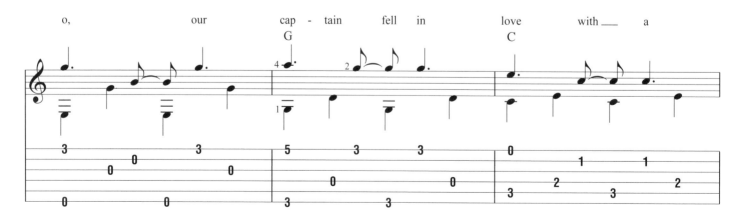

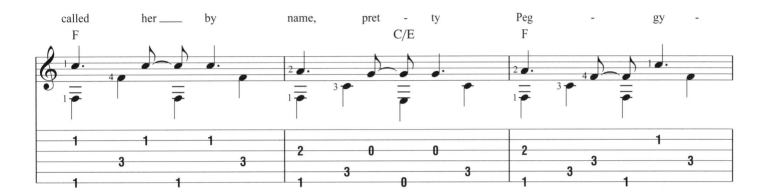

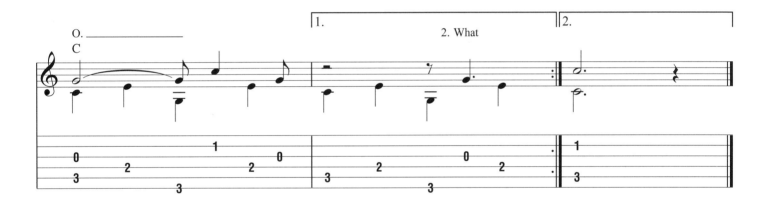

Additional Lyrics

2. What will your mother think, pretty Peggy-O?
   What will your mother think, pretty Peggy-O?
   What will your mother think when she hears the guineas clink,
   The soldiers all marching before you, oh?

Freight Train

Words and Music by Elizabeth Cotten

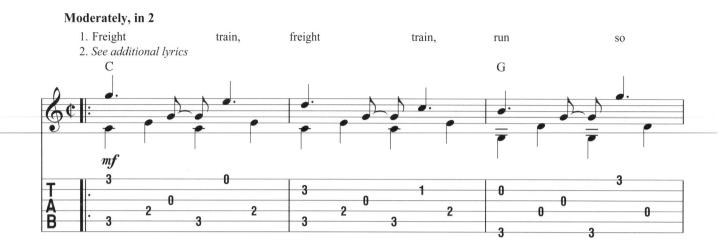

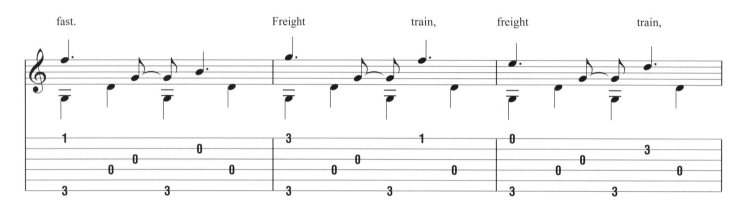

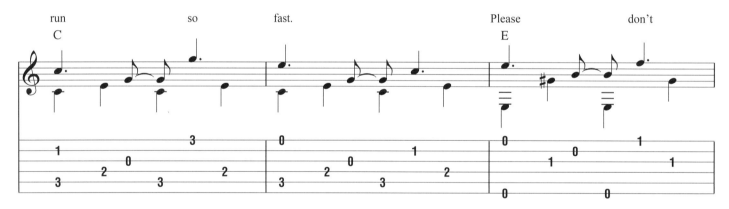

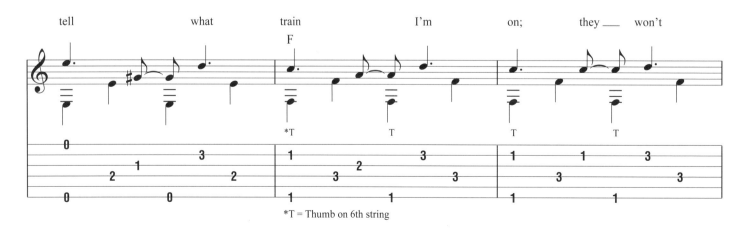

*T = Thumb on 6th string

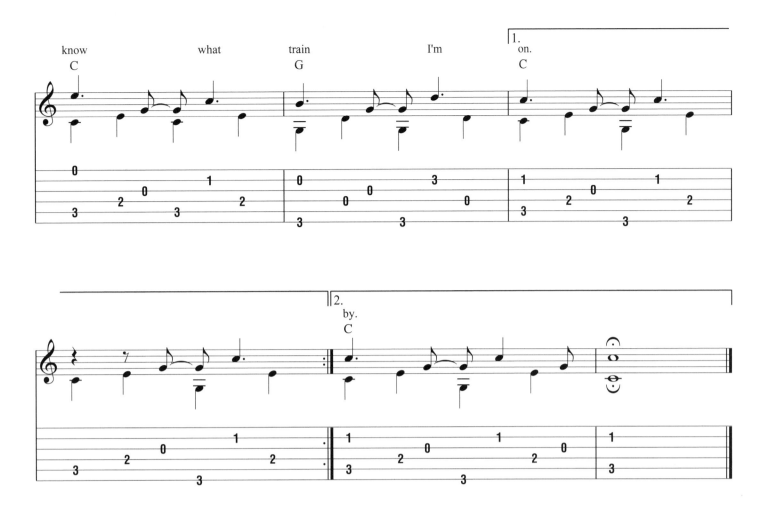

Additional Lyrics

2. When I die, Lord, bury me deep,
   Way down on old Chestnut Street.
   Then I can hear old Number Nine
   As she comes rolling by.

House of the Rising Sun

Southern American Folksong

Slowly, in 2

1. There is _____ a house _____ in

2. *See additional lyrics*

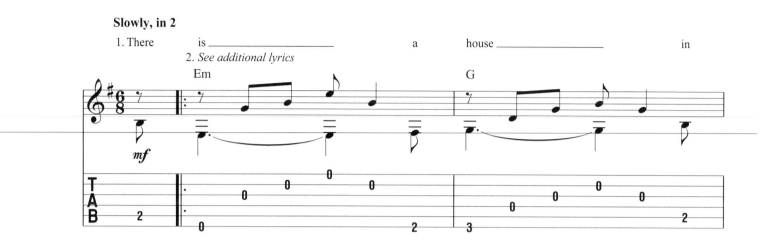

New _____ Or - leans _____ they call _____ the

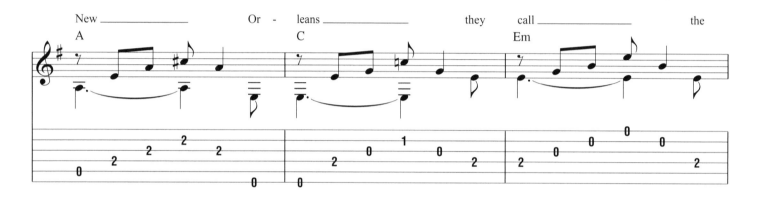

Ris - ing Sun. It's

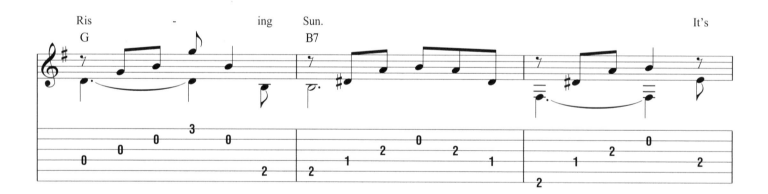

been _____ the ruin _____ of many a poor

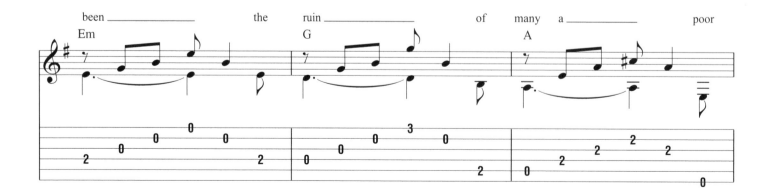

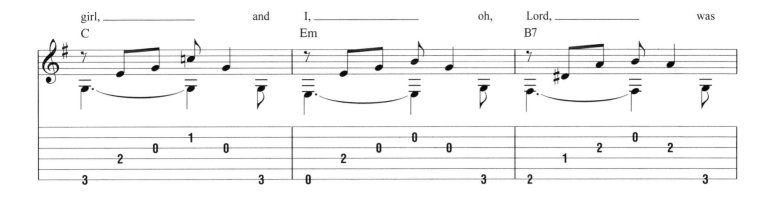

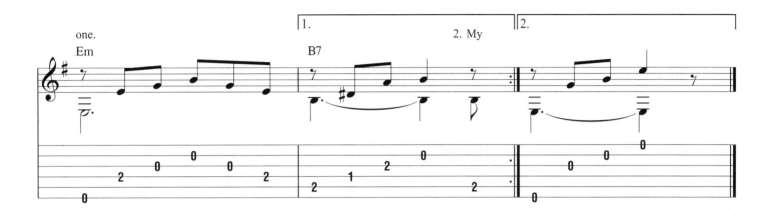

Additional Lyrics

2. My mother, she's a tailor;
   She sews those new blue jeans.
   My sweetheart, he's a drunkard, Lord,
   Drinks down in New Orleans.

I Gave My Love a Cherry
(The Riddle Song)
Traditional

Open D tuning:
(low to high) D-A-D-F#-A-D

Moderately, in 2

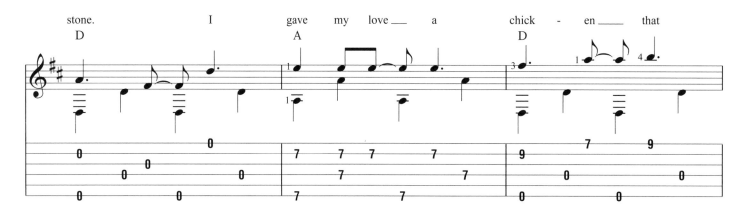

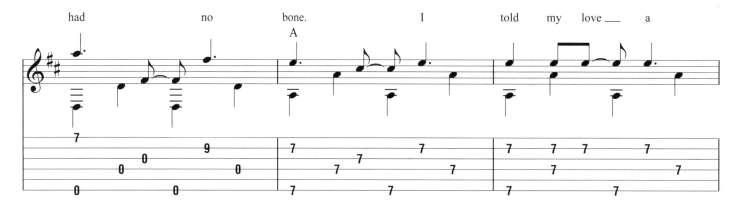

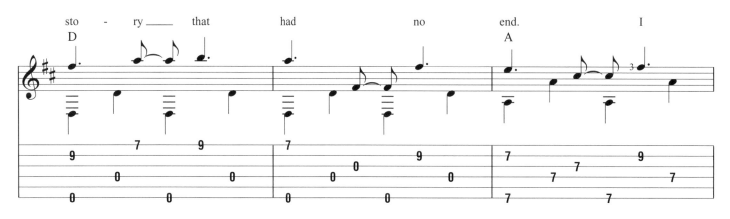

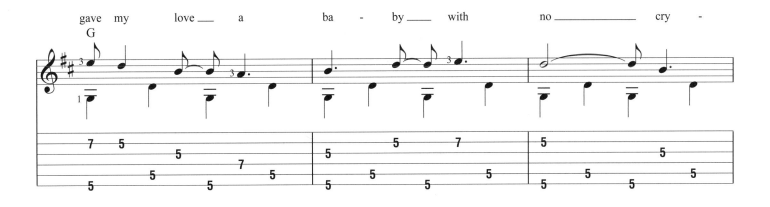

gave my love ___ a   ba - by ___ with   no _____ cry -

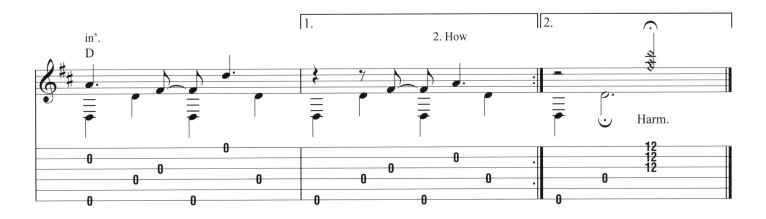

in'.

1.   2. How   2.   Harm.

Additional Lyrics

2. How can there be a cherry that has no stone?
   How can there be a chicken that has no bone?
   How can there be a story that has no end?
   How can there be a baby with no cryin'?

John Hardy

Traditional

Moderately, in 2

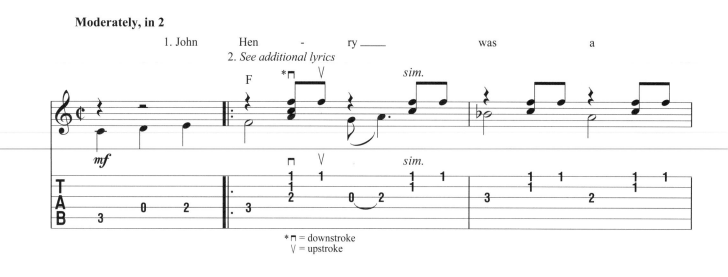

*⊓ = downstroke
∨ = upstroke

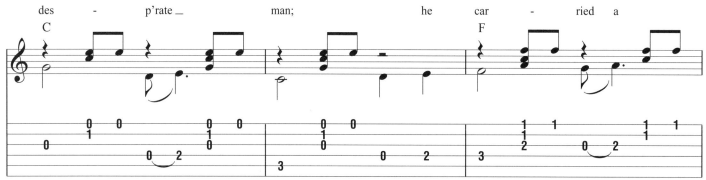

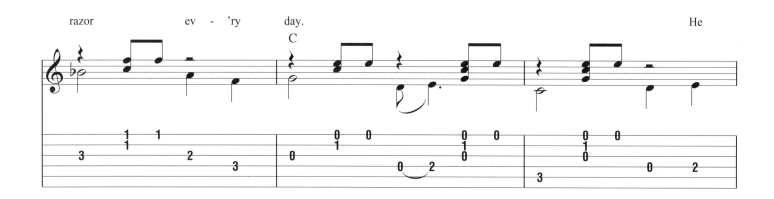

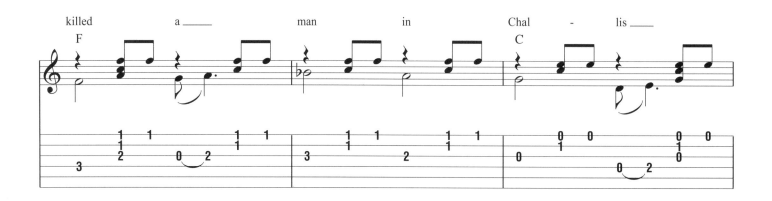

town.   You   ought to   see   poor   John - ny   get   a -

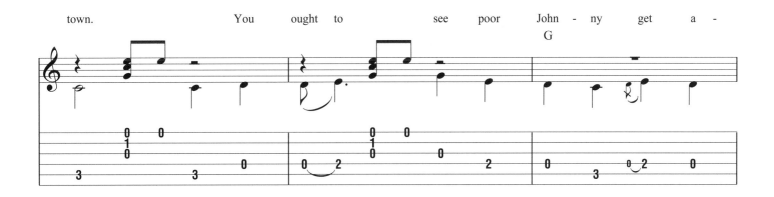

way.

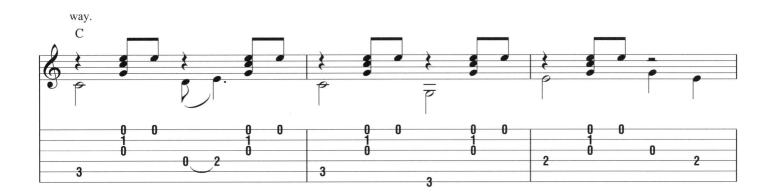

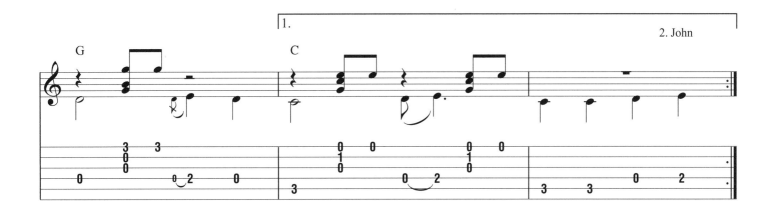

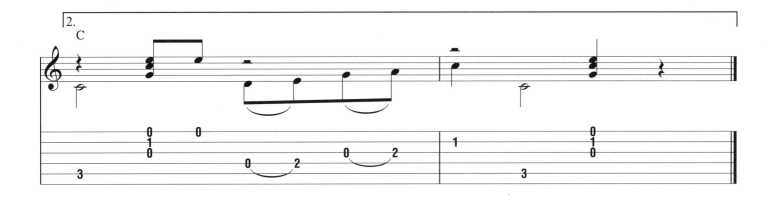

Additional Lyrics

2. John Henry went to the big, long town;
   He thought he was out of the way.
   Up stepped a marshall and took him by the hand,
   Says, "Johnny, come along with me."

29

John Henry

West Virginia Folksong

Moderately, in 2

1. When John Hen - ry was a lit - tle ba - by,
2. *See additional lyrics*

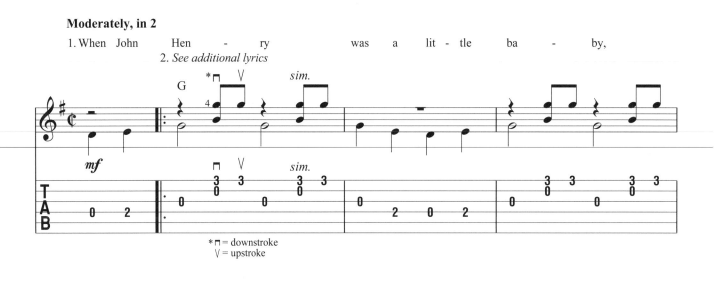

*☐ = downstroke
V = upstroke

sit - ting on his dad - dy's ___ .

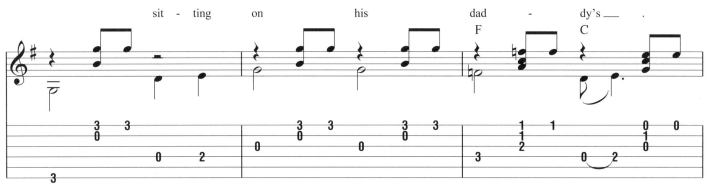

knee, he picked up a

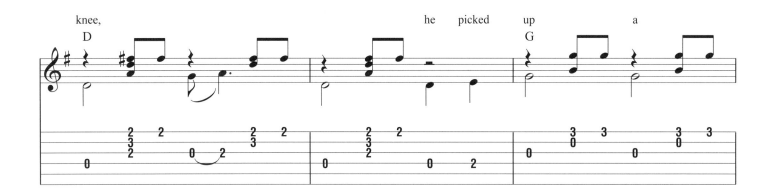

ham - mer and a little piece of steel, cried,

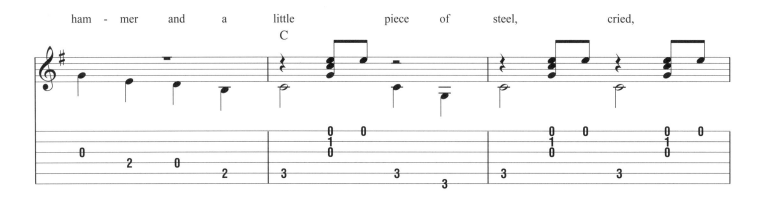

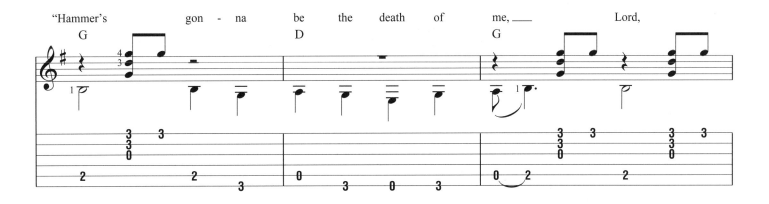

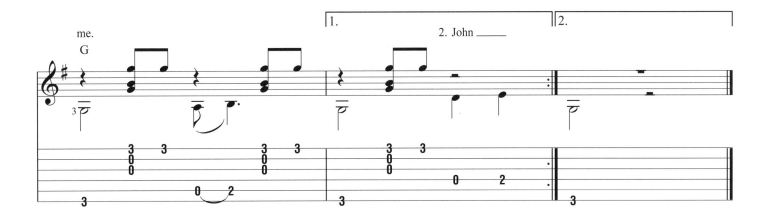

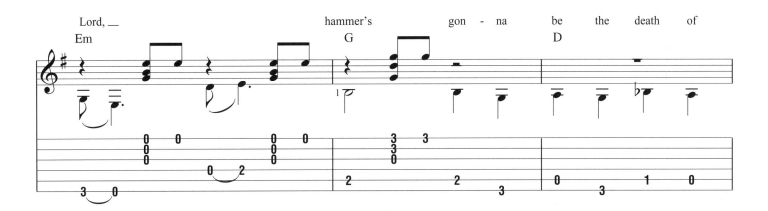

Additional Lyrics

2. John Henry said to his captain,
   "Gonna bring that steam drill 'round,
   Gonna bring that steam drill out on those tracks,
   Gonna knock that steel on down, God, God,
   Knock that steel on down."

Lily of the West

Traditional Irish

Moderately fast

1. When first I came to Lou - is - ville, some
2. *See additional lyrics*

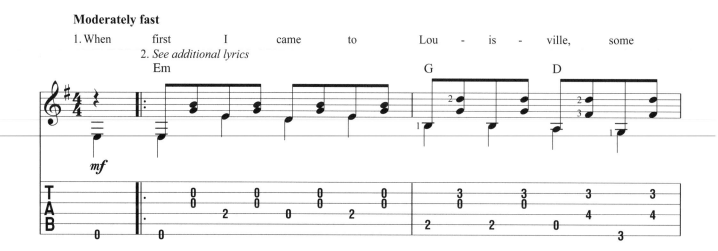

plea - sure there to find, a dam - sel there from

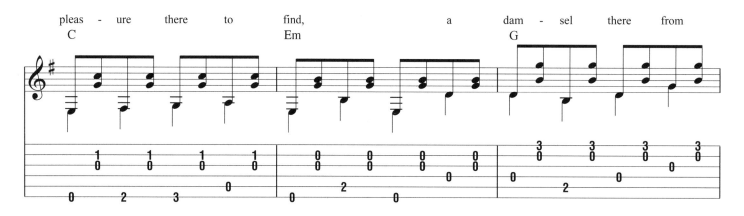

Lex - ing - ton was pleas - ing to my mind. Her

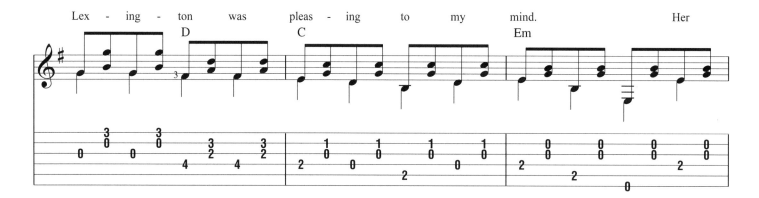

ros - y cheeks, her ru - by lips like ar - rows pierced my

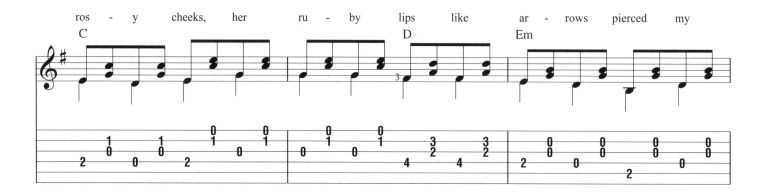

breast,   and the   name   she   bore   was   Flo - ra,   the

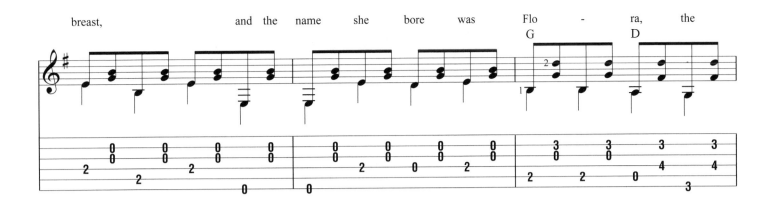

Lil - y   of   the   West.   2. I   West.

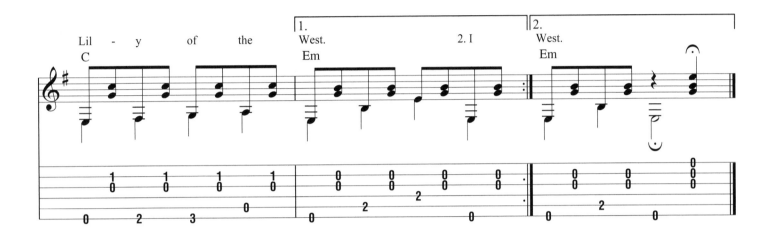

Additional Lyrics

2. I courted lovely Flora and to her I was so kind.
   But she went to another man, which sore distressed my mind.
   She robbed me of my liberty, deprived me of my rest.
   Betrayed was I by Flora, the Lily of the West.

The Lonesome Road

African-American Spiritual

Slowly, in 2

1. Look down, _____ look down _____ that lone - some

2. *See additional lyrics*

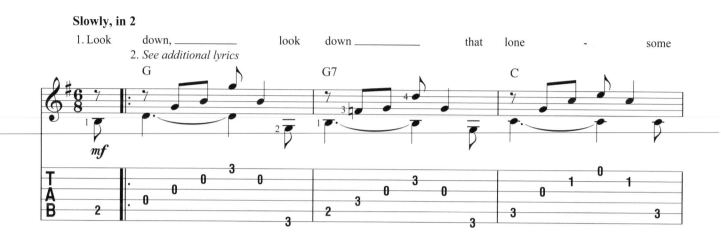

road; _____ hang down _____ your head _____ and

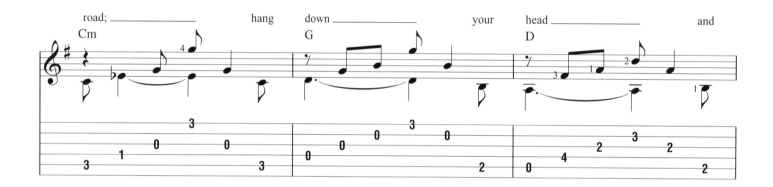

cry. _____ The best _____ of

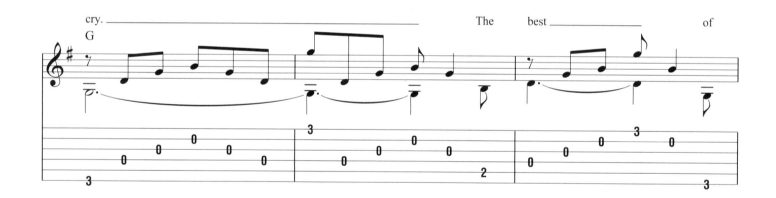

friends _____ must part _____ some day; _____ then

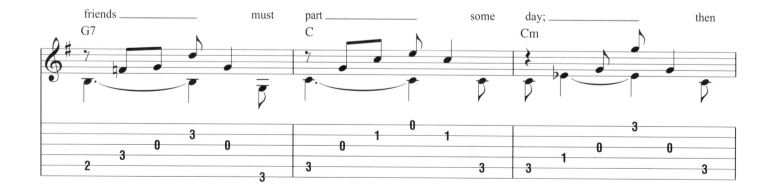

why _____ not you _____ and I?

2. True _____ fore.

Additional Lyrics

2. True love, true love, what have I done
   That you should treat me so?
   You caused me to talk and to walk with you
   Like I never done before.

Man of Constant Sorrow

Traditional

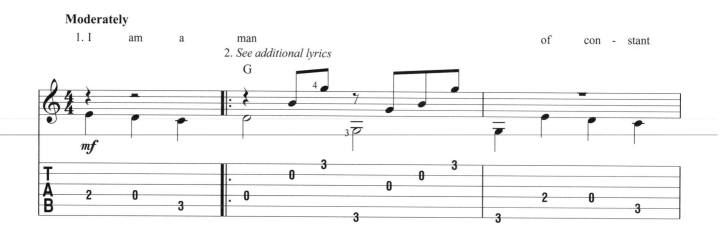

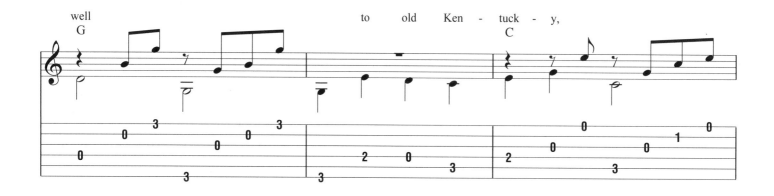

place   where   I   was   born ___ and

raised.   2. All   through   this

Additional Lyrics

2. All through this world I'm bound to ramble,
   Through sun and wind and driving rain.
   I'm bound to ride that northwest railway;
   Perhaps I'll take the very next train.

Matty Groves

English Folksong

Drop D tuning:
(low to high) D-A-D-G-B-E

Moderately, in 2

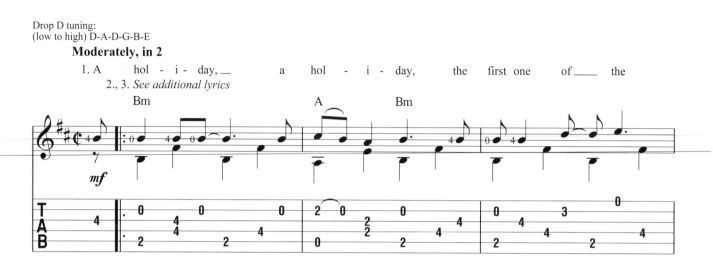

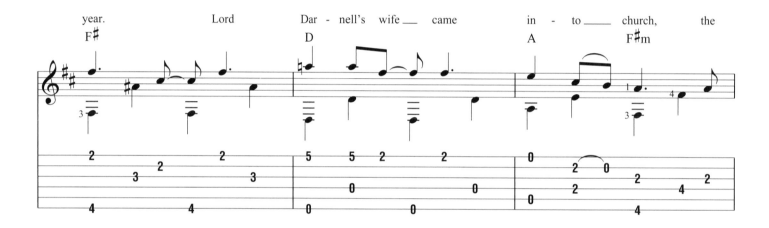

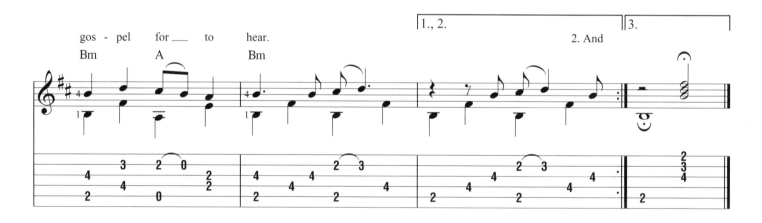

Additional Lyrics

2. And when the meeting, it was done, she cast her eyes about,
   And there she saw little Matty Groves walking in the crowd.

3. Come home with me, little Matty Groves, come home with me tonight.
   Come home with me, little Matty Groves, and sleep with me till light.

Michael Row the Boat Ashore

Traditional Folksong

Open D tuning:
(low to high) D-A-D-F#-A-D

Bright Calypso

1. Mi - chael, row the boat a - shore, hal - le -
2., 3. *See additional lyrics*

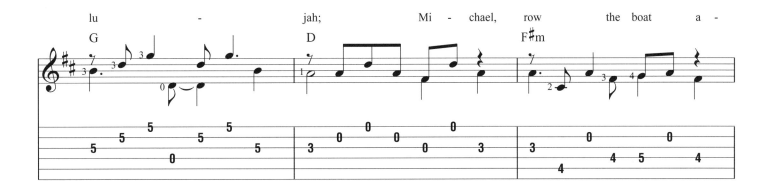

lu - jah; Mi - chael, row the boat a -

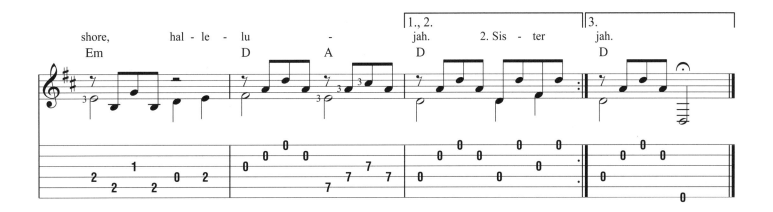

shore, hal - le - lu - jah. 2. Sis - ter jah.

Additional Lyrics

2. Sister help to trim the sails, hallelujah;
   Sister help to trim the sails, hallelujah

3. River Jordan is chilly and cold, hallelujah;
   Chills the body but not the soul, hallelujah.

Nine Hundred Miles

Traditional

Moderately, in 2

1. Well, I'm walk-ing down the track; __ I've got

2. *See additional lyrics*

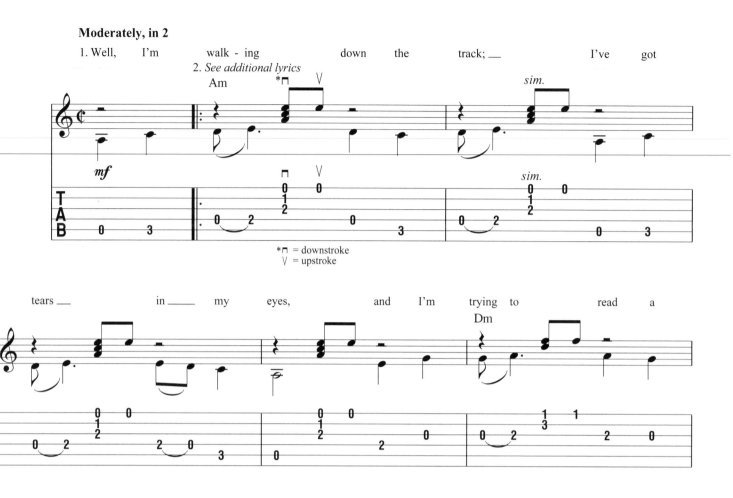

*⊓ = downstroke
V = upstroke

tears __ in __ my eyes, and I'm trying to read a

let - ter from my home. __ If that

train __ runs me right, I'll be home to - mor - row

night   'cause I'm   nine ____   hun - red   miles ____   from my

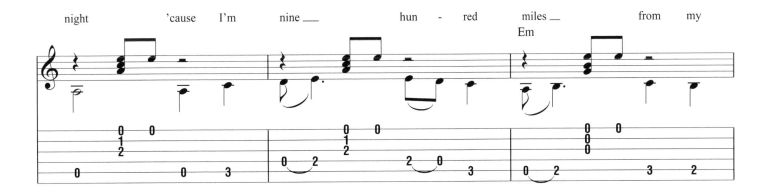

home,   and   I   hate to   hear that

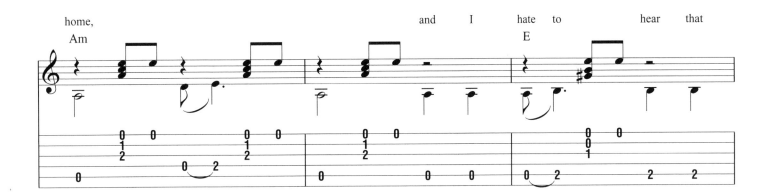

lone - some whis - tle   blow.   2. Well, this

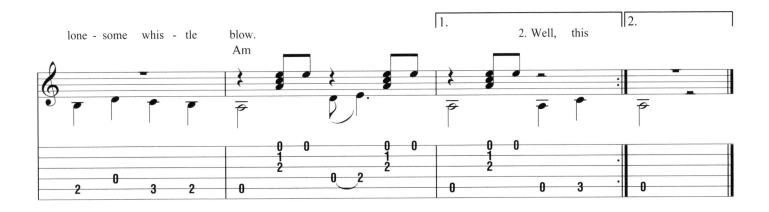

Additional Lyrics

2. Well, this train I ride on is a hundred coaches long.
You can hear the whistle blow a hundred miles.
If that train runs me right, I'll be home tomorrow night
'Cause I'm nine hundred miles from my home,
And I hate to hear that lonesome whistle blow.

Railroad Bill

Southern American Folksong

Drop D tuning:
(low to high) D-A-D-G-B-E

Moderately, in 2

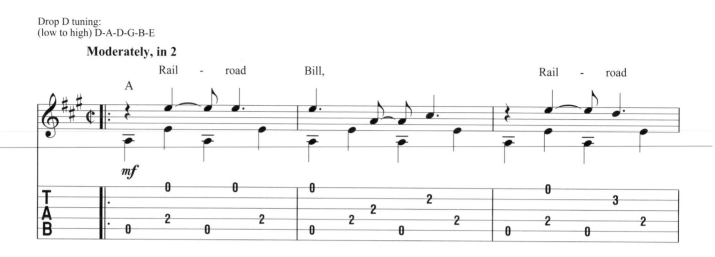

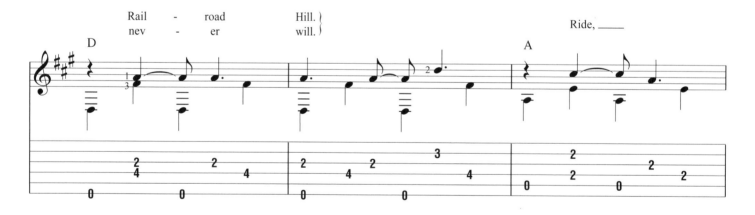

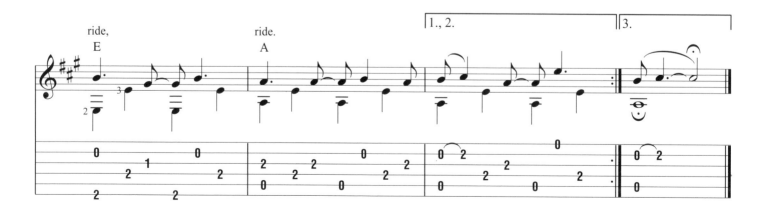

Shenandoah

American Folksong

Scarborough Fair

Traditional English

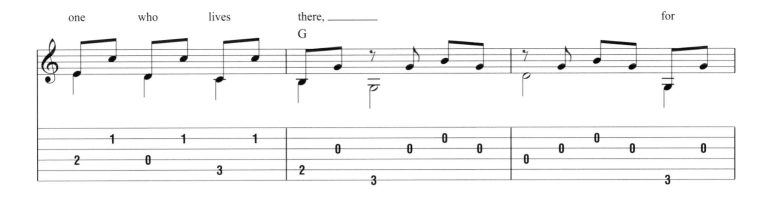

Additional Lyrics

2. Tell her to make me a cambric shirt,
   Parsley, sage, rosemary and thyme,
   Without any seam or fine needlework,
   For she once was a true love of mine.

Sloop John B.

Traditional

Open D tuning:
(low to high) D-A-D-F#-A-D

Bright Calypso

1. We come on the sloop John B., my
2. *See additional lyrics*

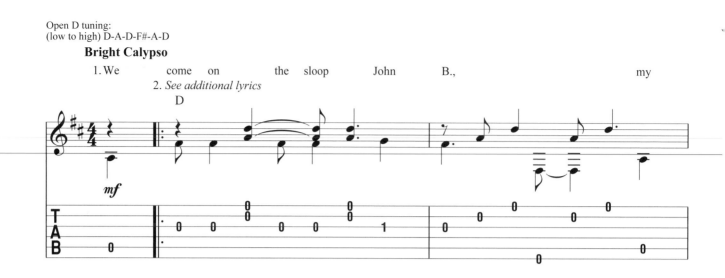

grand - fa - ther and me. A - round Nas - sau

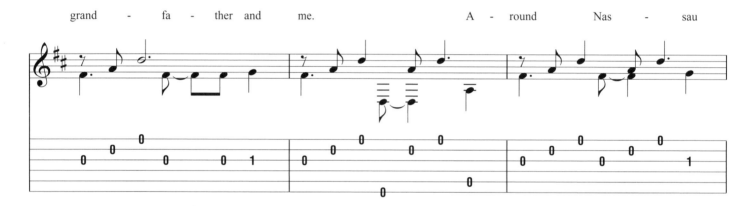

town we _____ did roam. Drink - ing all

night, got in - to a fight.

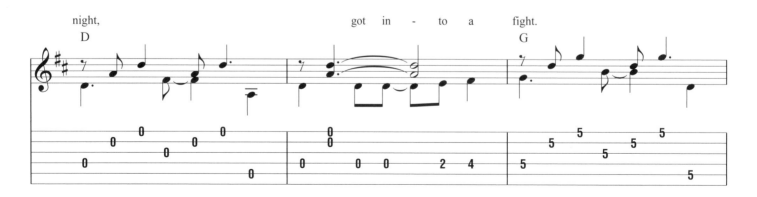

I feel so break ___ up; I wan - na go

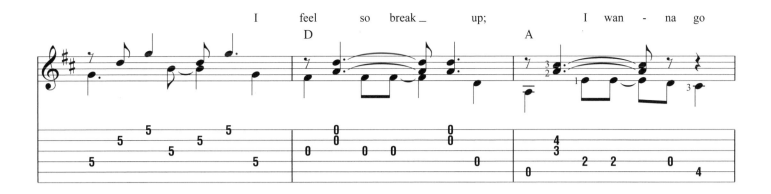

home.

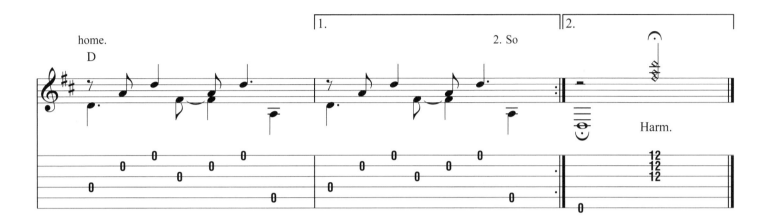

Harm.

Additional Lyrics

2. So hoist up the John B.'s sail; see how the mainsail sets.
   Call for the captain ashore; let me go home.
   Let me go home; I wanna go home.
   I feel so break up; I wanna go home.

Sometimes I Feel Like a Motherless Child

African-American Spiritual

Moderately, in 2

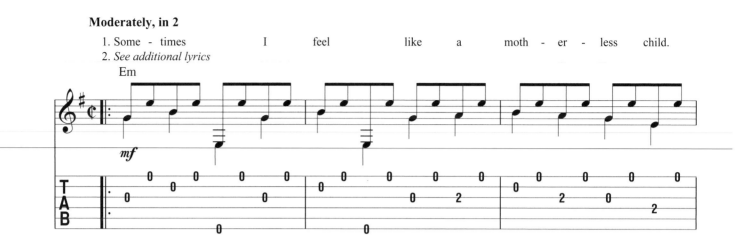

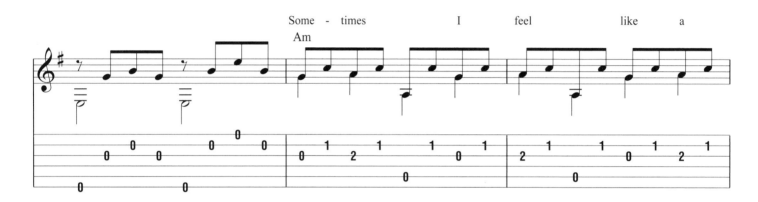

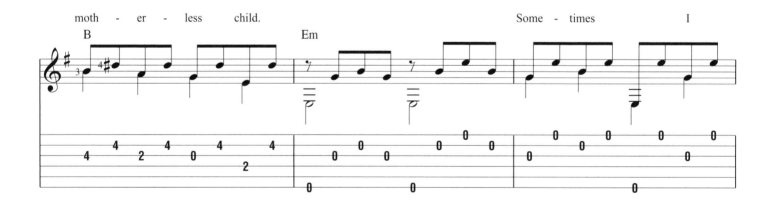

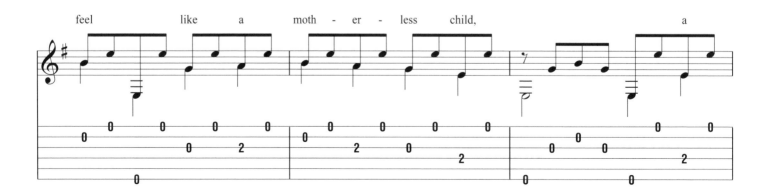

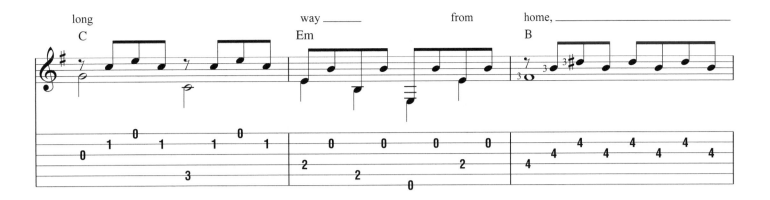

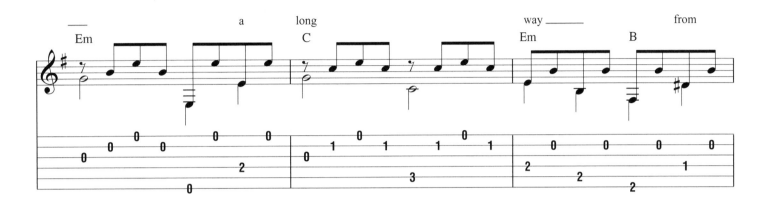

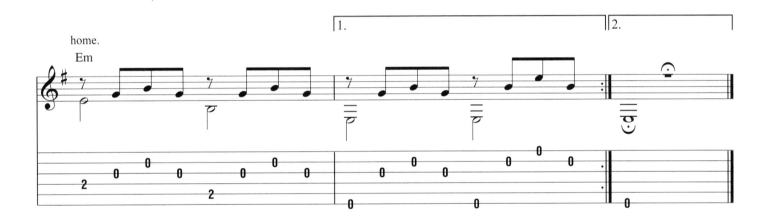

Additional Lyrics

2. Sometimes I feel like I'm almost gone.
Sometimes I feel like I'm almost gone.
Sometimes I feel like I'm almost gone,
A long way from home,
A long way from home.

The Streets of Laredo

American Cowboy Song

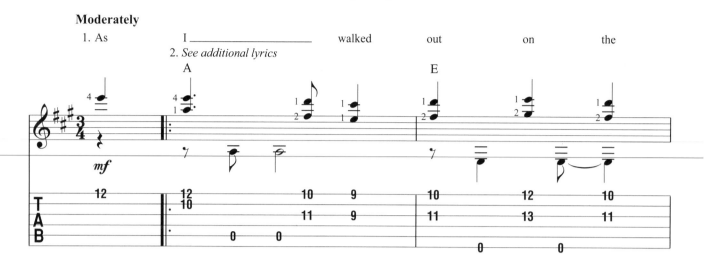

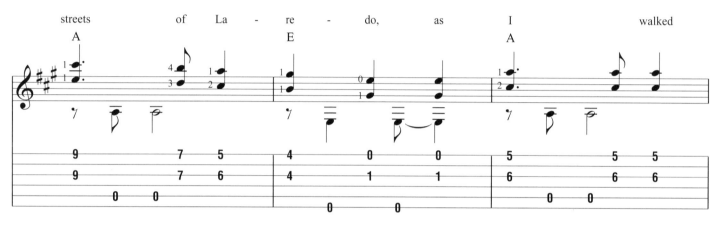

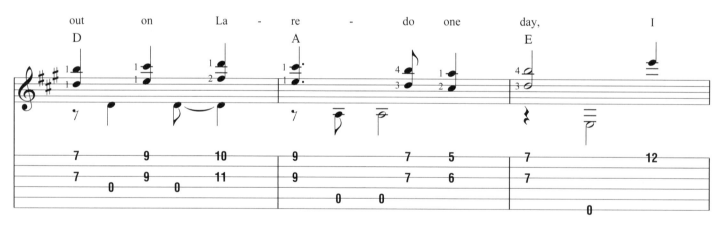

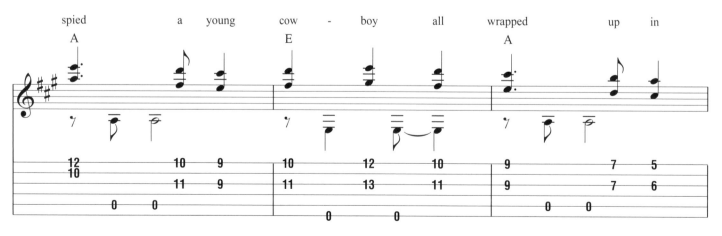

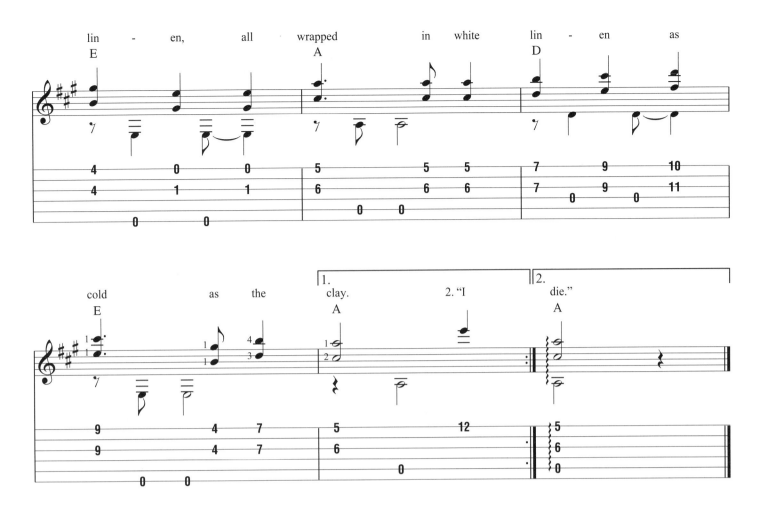

Additional Lyrics

2. "I see by your outfit that you are a cowboy."
   These words he did say as I proudly stepped by.
   "Come sit down beside me and hear my sad story.
   Got shot in the heart and I know I must die."

Tom Dooley

Traditional Folksong

Open D tuning:
(low to high) D-A-D-F#-A-D

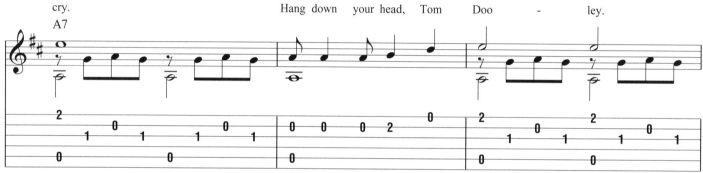

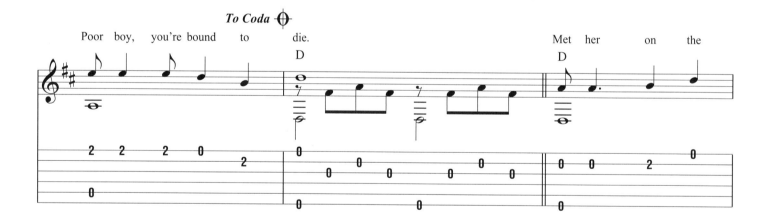

Met her on the moun - tain, stabbed her with my

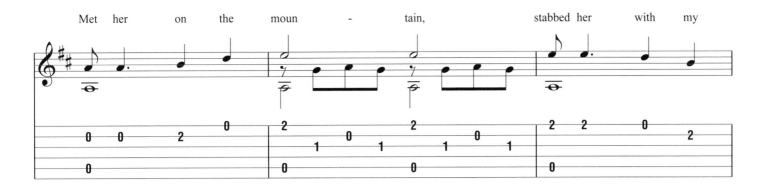

D.C. al Coda   ⊕ **Coda**

knife.   die.

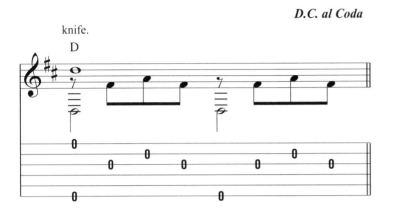

The Turtle Dove

English Folksong

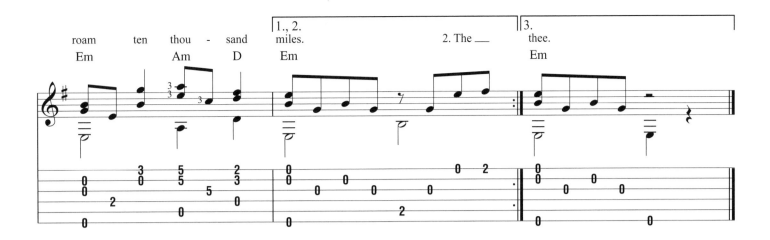

Additional Lyrics

2. The crow that is so black, my dear, shall change his color white.
   Before I'm false to the maiden I love, the noonday shall be night, my dear,
   The noonday shall be night.

3. Oh, don't you see yon turtle dove in yonder willow tree?
   She's weeping for her own true love as I shall weep for thee, my dear,
   As I shall weep for thee.

Water Is Wide

Traditional

Moderately

1. The wa - ter is wide;
2. *See additional lyrics*
I can - not get

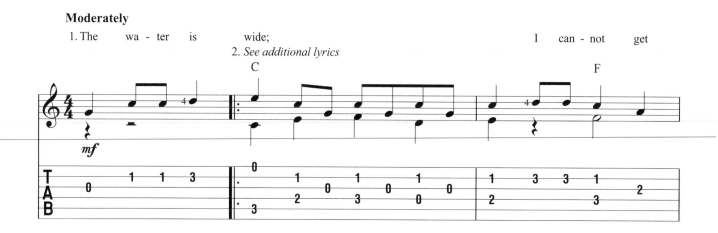

o'er.
Nei - ther have I

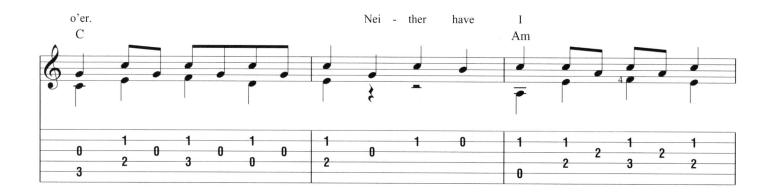

the wings to fly.
Give me a

boat
that can car - ry two,

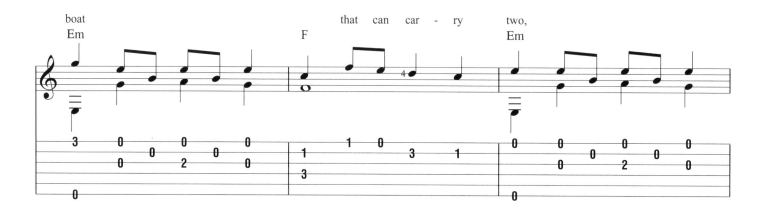

Additional Lyrics

2. There is a ship and she sails the sea.
   She's loaded deep as deep can be,
   But no so deep as the love I'm in.
   I know not how I sink or swim.

Wildwood Flower

Traditional

Open G tuning:
(low to high) D-G-D-G-B-D

Moderately, in 2

1. Oh, I'll twine with ___ my min - gles ___ and
2. *See additional lyrics*

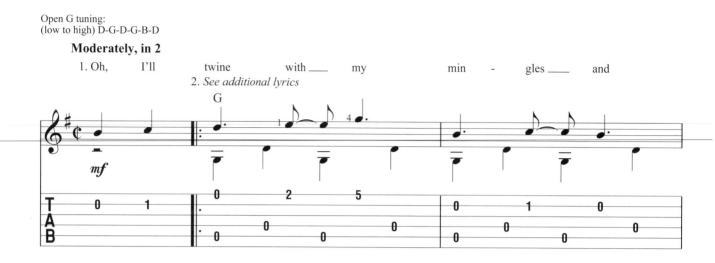

wav - ing ___ black hair, with ___ the

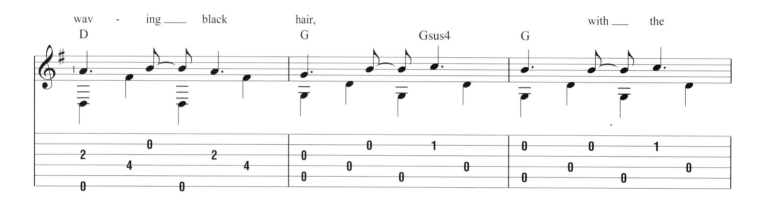

ros - es ___ so red and ___ the lil - ies ___ so

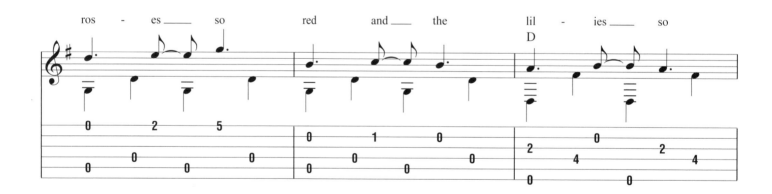

fair, and ___ the myr - tle ___ so

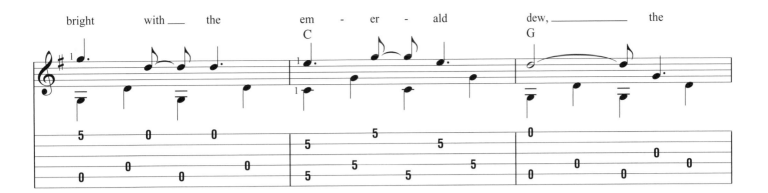

bright with ___ the   em - er - ald   dew, _____ the

pale   and ___ the   lead - er, ___ and   eyes   look ___ like

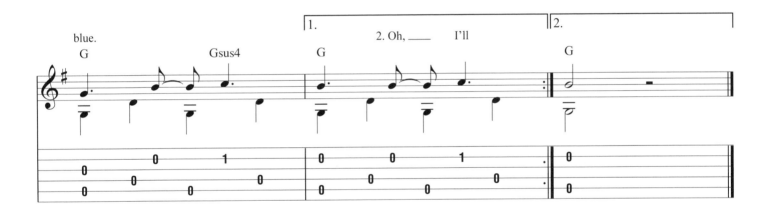

blue.

1.   2. Oh, ___   I'll   2.

Additional Lyrics

2. Oh, I'll dance, I will sing and my life shall be gay.
   I will charm every heart; in each crown I will sway.
   When I woke from my dreaming, my idols were clay.
   All portions of loving had all flown away.

FINGERPICKING GUITAR BOOKS

Hone your fingerpicking skills with these great songbooks featuring solo guitar arrangements in standard notation and tablature. The arrangements in these books are carefully written for intermediate-level guitarists. Each song combines melody and harmony in one superb guitar fingerpicking arrangement. Each book also includes an introduction to basic fingerstyle guitar.

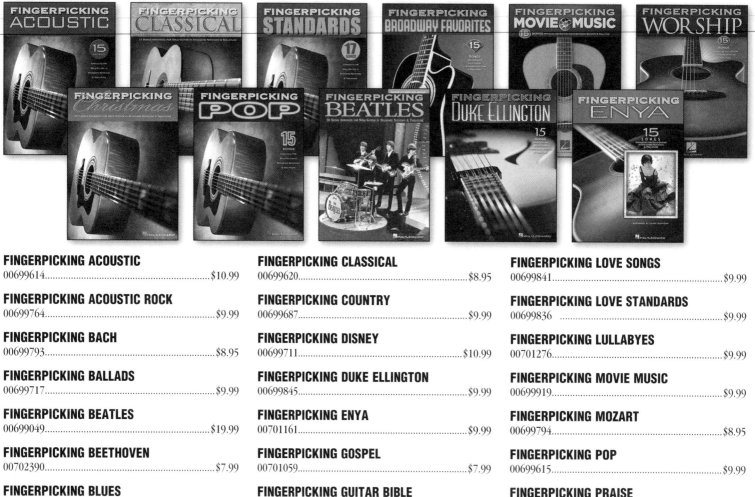

FINGERPICKING ACOUSTIC
00699614.................................$10.99

FINGERPICKING ACOUSTIC ROCK
00699764.................................$9.99

FINGERPICKING BACH
00699793.................................$8.95

FINGERPICKING BALLADS
00699717.................................$9.99

FINGERPICKING BEATLES
00699049.................................$19.99

FINGERPICKING BEETHOVEN
00702390.................................$7.99

FINGERPICKING BLUES
00701277.................................$7.99

FINGERPICKING BROADWAY FAVORITES
00699843.................................$9.99

FINGERPICKING BROADWAY HITS
00699838.................................$7.99

FINGERPICKING CELTIC FOLK
00701148.................................$7.99

FINGERPICKING CHILDREN'S SONGS
00699712.................................$9.99

FINGERPICKING CHRISTIAN
00701076.................................$7.99

FINGERPICKING CHRISTMAS
00699599.................................$9.99

FINGERPICKING CHRISTMAS CLASSICS
00701695.................................$7.99

FINGERPICKING CLASSICAL
00699620.................................$8.95

FINGERPICKING COUNTRY
00699687.................................$9.99

FINGERPICKING DISNEY
00699711.................................$10.99

FINGERPICKING DUKE ELLINGTON
00699845.................................$9.99

FINGERPICKING ENYA
00701161.................................$9.99

FINGERPICKING GOSPEL
00701059.................................$7.99

FINGERPICKING GUITAR BIBLE
00691040.................................$19.99

FINGERPICKING HYMNS
00699688.................................$8.95

FINGERPICKING IRISH SONGS
00701965.................................$7.99

FINGERPICKING JAZZ FAVORITES
00699844.................................$7.99

FINGERPICKING JAZZ STANDARDS
00699840.................................$7.99

FINGERPICKING LATIN FAVORITES
00699842.................................$9.99

FINGERPICKING LATIN STANDARDS
00699837.................................$7.99

FINGERPICKING ANDREW LLOYD WEBBER
00699839.................................$9.99

FINGERPICKING LOVE SONGS
00699841.................................$9.99

FINGERPICKING LOVE STANDARDS
00699836.................................$9.99

FINGERPICKING LULLABYES
00701276.................................$9.99

FINGERPICKING MOVIE MUSIC
00699919.................................$9.99

FINGERPICKING MOZART
00699794.................................$8.95

FINGERPICKING POP
00699615.................................$9.99

FINGERPICKING PRAISE
00699714.................................$8.95

FINGERPICKING ROCK
00699716.................................$10.99

FINGERPICKING STANDARDS
00699613.................................$9.99

FINGERPICKING WEDDING
00699637.................................$9.99

FINGERPICKING WORSHIP
00700554.................................$7.99

FINGERPICKING NEIL YOUNG – GREATEST HITS
00700134.................................$12.99

FINGERPICKING YULETIDE
00699654.................................$9.99

HAL•LEONARD® CORPORATION
7777 W. BLUEMOUND RD. P.O. BOX 13819 MILWAUKEE, WI 53213

Visit Hal Leonard online at **www.halleonard.com**

Prices, contents and availability subject to change without notice.

0915

AUTHENTIC CHORDS • ORIGINAL KEYS • COMPLETE SONGS

The *Strum It* series lets players strum the chords and sing along with their favorite hits. Each song has been selected because it can be played with regular open chords, barre chords, or other moveable chord types. Guitarists can simply play the rhythm, or play and sing along through the entire song. All songs are shown in their original keys complete with chords, strum patterns, melody and lyrics. Wherever possible, the chord voicings from the recorded versions are notated.

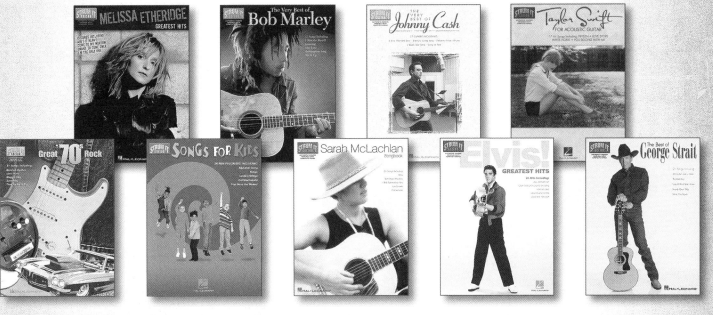

THE BEACH BOYS' GREATEST HITS
00699357... $12.95

THE BEATLES FAVORITES
00699249.....................................$14.95

BEST OF CONTEMPORARY CHRISTIAN
00699531.....................................$12.95

VERY BEST OF JOHNNY CASH
00699514.....................................$14.99

CELTIC GUITAR SONGBOOK
00699265.....................................$9.95

CHRISTMAS SONGS FOR GUITAR
00699247.....................................$10.95

CHRISTMAS SONGS WITH 3 CHORDS
00699487.....................................$8.95

VERY BEST OF ERIC CLAPTON
00699560.....................................$12.95

JIM CROCE – CLASSIC HITS
00699269.....................................$10.95

NEIL DIAMOND
00699593.....................................$12.95

DISNEY FAVORITES
00699171.....................................$10.95

MELISSA ETHERIDGE GREATEST HITS
00699518.....................................$12.99

FAVORITE SONGS WITH 3 CHORDS
00699112.....................................$8.95

FAVORITE SONGS WITH 4 CHORDS
00699270.....................................$8.95

FIRESIDE SING-ALONG
00699273.....................................$8.95

FOLK FAVORITES
00699517.....................................$8.95

THE GUITAR STRUMMERS' ROCK SONGBOOK
00701678.....................................$14.99

BEST OF WOODY GUTHRIE
00699496.....................................$12.95

JOHN HIATT COLLECTION
00699398.....................................$12.95

THE VERY BEST OF BOB MARLEY
00699524.....................................$12.95

A MERRY CHRISTMAS SONGBOOK
00699211.....................................$9.95

MORE FAVORITE SONGS WITH 3 CHORDS
00699532.....................................$8.95

THE VERY BEST OF TOM PETTY
00699336.....................................$12.95

POP-ROCK GUITAR FAVORITES
00699088.....................................$8.95

ELVIS! GREATEST HITS
00699276.....................................$10.95

BEST OF GEORGE STRAIT
00699235.....................................$14.99

TAYLOR SWIFT FOR ACOUSTIC GUITAR
00109717.....................................$16.99

BEST OF HANK WILLIAMS JR.
00699224.....................................$14.99

HAL•LEONARD®
7777 W. BLUEMOUND RD. P.O. BOX 13819
MILWAUKEE, WISCONSIN 53213

Prices, contents & availability subject to change without notice.

Visit Hal Leonard online at
www.halleonard.com

0316

Guitar Chord Songbooks

Each 6" x 9" book includes complete lyrics, chord symbols, and guitar chord diagrams.

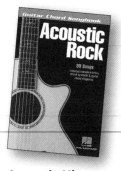

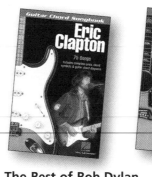

Acoustic Hits
00701787 . . . . $14.99

Acoustic Rock
00699540 . . . . $17.95

Adele
00102761 . . . . $14.99

Alabama
00699914 . . . . $14.95

The Beach Boys
00699566 . . . . $14.95

The Beatles (A-I)
00699558 . . . . $17.99

The Beatles (J-Y)
00699562 . . . . $17.99

Bluegrass
00702585 . . . . $14.99

Broadway
00699920 . . . . $14.99

Johnny Cash
00699648 . . . . $17.99

Steven Curtis Chapman
00700702 . . . . $17.99

Children's Songs
00699539 . . . . $16.99

Christmas Carols
00699536 . . . . $12.99

Christmas Songs – 2nd Edition
00119911 . . . . $14.99

Eric Clapton
00699567 . . . . $15.99

Classic Rock
00699598 . . . . $15.99

Coffeehouse Hits
00703318 . . . . $14.99

Country
00699534 . . . . $14.99

Country Favorites
00700609 . . . . $14.99

Country Hits
00140859 . . . . $14.99

Country Standards
00700608 . . . . $12.95

Cowboy Songs
00699636 . . . . $12.95

Creedence Clearwater Revival
00701786 . . . . $12.99

Crosby, Stills & Nash
00701609 . . . . $12.99

John Denver
02501697 . . . . $14.99

Neil Diamond
00700606 . . . . $14.99

Disney
00701071 . . . . $14.99

The Best of Bob Dylan
14037617 . . . . $17.99

Eagles
00122917 . . . . $16.99

Early Rock
00699916 . . . . $14.99

Folksongs
00699541 . . . . $14.99

Folk Pop Rock
00699651 . . . . $14.95

40 Easy Strumming Songs
00115972 . . . . $14.99

Four Chord Songs
00701611 . . . . $12.99

Glee
00702501 . . . . $14.99

Gospel Hymns
00700463 . . . . $14.99

Grand Ole Opry®
00699885 . . . . $16.95

Grateful Dead
00139461 . . . . $14.99

Green Day
00103074 . . . . $12.99

Guitar Chord Songbook White Pages
00702609 . . . . $29.99

Irish Songs
00701044 . . . . $14.99

Michael Jackson
00137847 . . . . $14.99

Billy Joel
00699632 . . . . $15.99

Elton John
00699732 . . . . $15.99

Ray LaMontagne
00130337 . . . . $12.99

Latin Songs
00700973 . . . . $14.99

Love Songs
00701043 . . . . $14.99

Bob Marley
00701704 . . . . $12.99

Bruno Mars
00125332 . . . . $12.99

Paul McCartney
00385035 . . . . $16.95

Steve Miller
00701146 . . . . $12.99

Prices, contents, and availability subject to change without notice.

Modern Worship
00701801 . . . . $16.99

Motown
00699734 . . . . $16.95

The 1950s
00699922 . . . . $14.99

The 1980s
00700551 . . . . $16.99

Nirvana
00699762 . . . . $16.99

Roy Orbison
00699752 . . . . $12.95

Peter, Paul & Mary
00103013 . . . . $12.99

Tom Petty
00699883 . . . . $15.99

Pink Floyd
00139116 . . . . $14.99

Pop/Rock
00699538 . . . . $14.95

Praise & Worship
00699634 . . . . $14.99

Elvis Presley
00699633 . . . . $14.95

Queen
00702395 . . . . $12.99

Rascal Flatts
00130951 . . . . $12.99

Red Hot Chili Peppers
00699710 . . . . $16.95

Rock Ballads
00701034 . . . . $14.99

The Rolling Stones
00137716 . . . . $14.99

Bob Seger
00701147 . . . . $12.99

Carly Simon
00121011 . . . . $14.99

Singer/Songwriter Songs
00126053 . . . . $14.99

Sting
00699921 . . . . $14.99

Taylor Swift
00701799 . . . . $15.99

Three Chord Acoustic Songs
00123860 . . . . $14.99

Three Chord Songs
00699720 . . . . $12.95

Today's Hits
00120983 . . . . $14.99

Top 100 Hymns Guitar Songbook
75718017 . . . . $14.99

Two-Chord Songs
00119236 . . . . $14.99

Ultimate-Guitar
00702617 . . . . $24.99

U2
00137744 . . . . $14.99

Wedding Songs
00701005 . . . . $14.99

Hank Williams
00700607 . . . . $14.99

Stevie Wonder
00120862 . . . . $14.99

Neil Young–Decade
00700464 . . . . $14.99

0316

STRUM & SING

Lyrics, chord symbols, and guitar chord diagrams for your favorite songs.

GUITAR

SARA BAREILLES
00102354.........................$12.99

ZAC BROWN BAND
02501620.........................$12.99

COLBIE CAILLAT
02501725.........................$14.99

CAMPFIRE FOLK SONGS
02500686.........................$10.99

CHART HITS OF 2014-2015
00142554.........................$12.99

BEST OF KENNY CHESNEY
00142457.........................$14.99

KELLY CLARKSON
00146384.........................$14.99

JOHN DENVER COLLECTION
02500632.........................$9.95

EAGLES
00157994.........................$12.99

EASY ACOUSTIC SONGS
00125478.........................$12.99

50 CHILDREN'S SONGS
02500825.........................$7.95

THE 5 CHORD SONGBOOK
02501718.........................$10.99

FOLK SONGS
02501482.........................$9.99

FOLK/ROCK FAVORITES
02501669.........................$9.99

40 POP/ROCK HITS
02500633.........................$9.95

THE 4 CHORD SONGBOOK
02501533.........................$12.99

THE 4-CHORD COUNTRY SONGBOOK
00114936.........................$12.99

HITS OF THE '60S
02501138.........................$10.95

HITS OF THE '70S
02500871.........................$9.99

HYMNS
02501125.........................$8.99

JACK JOHNSON
02500858.........................$16.99

CAROLE KING
00115243.........................$10.99

BEST OF GORDON LIGHTFOOT
00139393.........................$14.99

DAVE MATTHEWS BAND
02501078.........................$10.95

JOHN MAYER
02501636.........................$10.99

INGRID MICHAELSON
02501634.........................$10.99

THE MOST REQUESTED SONGS
02501748.........................$10.99

JASON MRAZ
02501452.........................$14.99

PRAISE & WORSHIP
00152381.........................$12.99

ROCK AROUND THE CLOCK
00103625.........................$12.99

ROCK BALLADS
02500872.........................$9.95

ED SHEERAN
00152016.........................$12.99

THE 6 CHORD SONGBOOK
02502277.........................$10.99

CAT STEVENS
00116827.........................$10.99

TODAY'S HITS
00119301.........................$10.99

KEITH URBAN
00118558.........................$12.99

NEIL YOUNG – GREATEST HITS
00138270.........................$12.99

UKULELE

COLBIE CAILLAT
02501731.........................$10.99

JOHN DENVER
02501694.........................$10.99

JACK JOHNSON
02501702.........................$15.99

JOHN MAYER
02501706.........................$10.99

INGRID MICHAELSON
02501741.........................$10.99

THE MOST REQUESTED SONGS
02501453.........................$14.99

JASON MRAZ
02501753.........................$14.99

SING-ALONG SONGS
02501710.........................$14.99

www.halleonard.com
Visit our website to see full song lists.

HAL•LEONARD® CORPORATION

7777 W. Bluemound Rd. P.O. Box 13819 Milwaukee, WI 53213

Prices, content, and availability subject to change without notice.

0316

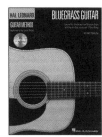

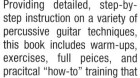